ABOUT THIS NO NONSENSE STUDY GUIDE™

This No Nonsense Study Guide, like each Study Guide, has been designed to live up to *both* parts of its name . . . to provide you with useful No Nonsense information *and* to increase your personal chances for Student Success!

Term papers, like pop quizzes and achievement tests, typically cause stress among virtually all students without regard to class ranking.

The primary purpose of this book is to reduce and hopefully eliminate your basic fear of term papers.

The most effective method of achieving this objective is to make the process of researching and writing a term paper as comfortable and fear-free as possible.

This straight-speaking guide has been designed to help you to clearly understand, organize and successfully complete the process so that you will be in a position to make your next term paper a winning one!

THE NO NONSENSE LIBRARY™

NO NONSENSE SUCCESS GUIDES

The Self-Employment Test
Getting Into The Mail Order Business
How To Run A Business Out Of Your Home
How To Own and Operate A Franchise
How (and Where) To Get The Money To Get Started
Getting Into The Consulting Business

NO NONSENSE FINANCIAL GUIDES

NO NONSENSE CAREER GUIDES

NO NONSENSE REAL ESTATE GUIDES

NO NONSENSE LEGAL GUIDES

NO NONSENSE HEALTH GUIDES

NO NONSENSE COOKING GUIDES

NO NONSENSE WINE GUIDES

NO NONSENSE PARENTING GUIDES

NO NONSENSE STUDY GUIDES

How To Write A Winning Term Paper
The Parent-Student Guide To
Selecting Colleges & Universities

NO NONSENSE

STUDY GUIDE™

HOW TO WRITE A WINNING TERM PAPER

STEVE KAHN

LONGMEADOW PRESS

How To Write A Winning Term Paper

Cover design by Tom Fowler, Inc.

Composition by Tod Clonan Associates, Inc.

Published by Longmeadow Press, 201 High Ridge Road, Stamford, Connecticut 06904.

ISBN: 0-681-40445-0

Printed in the United States of America

0 9 8 7 6 5 4 3 2 1

TABLE OF CONTENTS

HOW TO USE THIS BOOK

In order for your term papers to succeed, you must succeed in proving your premise: The central theme or question which forms the basis of your assignment.

This entire book is devoted and designed to help you achieve this single basic objective.

If you can achieve it, and I am confident that you can, you will never again be intimidated by the assignment of a term paper.

This book is written for high school students and college undergraduates.

At times, some of the information may seem familiar. However, even superstar athletes practice their fundamentals each day; in school, as well as in sports, fundamentals form the foundation of sustained success.

Our suggestion is to read this book once *without* taking notes or making decisions.

Then put it aside until your next term paper assignment.

By that time, this book should be as comfortable as a good friend, at your side to help you organize, research, write and hand in a winning term paper.

After all, that's what friends are for!

CHAPTER

1

WHAT EXACTLY IS A TERM PAPER

Term paper.

From a teacher's point of view, it's simply another assignment.

From most students' point of view, it's not unlike being sentenced to an involuntary term of hard labor.

From our point of view, it's an academic activity which *can* be performed without undue stress or unfounded fear.

Therefore, this book is founded upon three very clear objectives:

(1) To help you to plan, research and write successful term papers.

(2) To reduce and hopefully eliminate your anxiety about term papers.

(3) To help you to discover that producing term papers actually can be fun or, at the very least, painless.

Is A Term Paper The Same As A Research Paper Or A Thesis Or A Dissertation?

Yes and no.

A term paper can, in fact, properly be characterized as a research paper. Research, according to *The American Heritage Dictionary*, is a "careful study of a subject." That could also be the definition of a successful term paper.

Typically, a term paper is a research paper assigned to fulfill the requirements of a high school or college undergraduate course. A thesis is typically in fulfillment of a graduate master's degree, and a dissertation is in fulfillment of a doctoral candidacy.

All of them are defined as research papers. However, their complexity and scope increase as the level of scholarship increases.

Research, at every level, requires a methodical, complete and accurate study of the assigned subject matter. You will not succeed in proving the premise of your paper unless you have thoroughly researched the subject.

Thus, even as a high school student or college undergraduate, your challenge will be to produce successful term papers.

They will succeed only if your research is complete, comprehensive and, ultimately, convincing.

A Term Paper Is Both A Challenge And An Opportunity

Every term paper begins the same way a great novel begins: with a stack of blank pages, an open mind and the challenge to combine the two in a way that will fill those pages with information that will capture and hold the attention of your audience (in this instance, your teacher).

In meeting this challenge, you are given an equally compelling opportunity. In fact, you are given *three* opportunities.

(1) The opportunity to discipline yourself, and your writing, as you focus on a particular subject. It will be a single-minded exercise in concentrating on a single subject; you will be like a jeweler seeking to capture all of the facets of a solitary diamond; only your skill and imagination will determine the value of the diamond; it can remain a "diamond in the rough" or become a bright and beautiful piece.

(2) The opportunity to learn where to find, and how to use, the many resources which are available to researchers. You will be surprised at the vast and helpful amount of information within your grasp.

(3) The opportunity to become an expert on a subject. It's a good feeling to become confidently knowledgeable about a subject. The process of producing a term paper will provide you with that knowledge — and good feeling.

The One Characteristic Which Distinguishes A Term Paper From Less Formal Writings

That characteristic is documentation.

As the writer of a term paper, you will be required to document all of the sources which you used to produce your paper. They may include books, magazines, encyclopedias, television programs, even compact discs.

That clearly distinguishes it, for example, from a book report, which is based on a single source. You will use many sources for a term paper, and you will be required to document each of them.

All of your sources must be acknowledged in your bibliography, which is the subject of chapter seven.

Along the way, throughout the paper, you will also be required to footnote; that is, to indicate within the body of the text those sources responsible for a particular piece of information, a specific quotation, etc.

Footnotes are the subject of chapter ten.

Consider Yourself A Lawyer Who Has To Convince A Jury

Like a lawyer setting out to prove his case, as the writer of a term paper you will be faced with a similar set of circumstances.

Your term paper, like the lawyer's opening remarks to the judge or jury, will begin with a statement setting out your premise and how you intend to establish and prove that premise.

Your premise — the central theme of your term paper — is the key to the assignment. We have already said it and will say it again: Your term paper will only succeed if you can convincingly prove your premise.

Consider your premise to be your guiding compass (or road map), and keep checking it to make certain that you are moving forward in the right direction.

That means that your facts, sources, data and personal observations must clearly, logically and accurately be combined to effectively present and prove your premise.

Thus, the heart of your paper, like the lawyer's persuasive arguments, will be to convincingly present all of the evidence which you have collected in support of your premise.

Your conclusion, like the lawyer's closing arguments, will summarize why you believe that you have succeeded in proving your premise.

Like a winning verdict from a judge or jury, a successful term paper will provide you with even greater confidence for your next assignment.

If the topic for your term paper is determined by your teacher, you can skip this chapter.

If you have no part in the selection process, the only suggestion we would make is that if, for one reason or another, you find the preselected topic unreasonable or uncomfortable, you should arrange for a conference with your teacher as quickly as possible.

You might be able to modify the assignment or be provided with an alternative topic more to your liking.

You might also be stuck with the original subject matter. In that case, our only observation would be that life isn't perfect and that, by the time you've completed your paper, you might be pleasantly surprised that it wasn't as terrible as you feared.

More often than not, however, you *will* have some choices in the selection of the topic for a term paper.

Your opportunity to participate in the selection process is

obviously a plus; however, making that selection will not be as simple as it might seem.

Too Broad A Topic

A common tendency is to select a sweeping topic which exceeds the more modest scope of a term paper.

Examples might be:

The History of Baseball.

The Vietnam War.

The Works of Shakespeare.

Full-length books could hardly do justice to topics of this magnitude.

For the purpose of a term paper, these three examples might be narrowed as follows:

Did Abner Doubleday Really Invent Baseball?

How The Gulf of Tonkin Resolution Changed The Course of American Involvement in The Vietnam War.

A Comparison of Hamlet and King Lear.

The topic which you select has to be carefully and closely defined so that you can prove and present it within a reasonable length without losing your credibility or the reader's interest.

Too Narrow A Topic

Selecting a topic which is too narrow can also cause difficulties.

There are, of course, some exceptions to this rule. For example, *November 22, 1963: The Day John F. Kennedy*

Was Assassinated.

A topic such as *Why Chicago Is Called 'The Windy City'*, however, might give a teacher pause — and give you a problem in producing an adequate paper.

A Topic For Which Research Material Is Available

The key to the success of your term paper will obviously combine the quality and quantity of your research together with your skill in distilling and delineating that information in an interesting and credible manner.

You will be at a serious disadvantage if there is only limited information available regarding the topic which you have selected.

Therefore, before making a final selection, make certain that there is sufficient information available to enable you to produce a complete and thoroughly documented paper.

A Topic Of Interest To You

Excitement is contagious. If you like something, whether it's a piece of music or a piece of clothing, your positive feelings joyfully rise to the surface and can quickly be shared by those around you.

The excitement which you can bring to the production of a term paper can be equally contagious; good teachers truly love to share the enthusiasm of their students.

Thus, you should try to find a topic which excites you or, at least, seriously interests you.

It will give you a head start in the process, and a serious advantage over other papers written by students who selected their topics at the last minute or by rote. More importantly, it will make the term paper process more enjoyable and bearable for you.

A Topic Within Your Expertise

While a term paper is ideally an assignment designed to expand your knowledge, it should not become an unreasonable burden.

By this, we are not suggesting that you take any short cuts or otherwise shirk your responsibilities as an honorable and productive student. We are, however, suggesting that you select a topic with which you feel intellectually comfortable.

If you have a term paper assignment in physics, for example, and certain aspects of the subject have always been particularly difficult for you, you should probably *not* select a topic dealing with those elusive aspects.

Give yourself every possible advantage within the framework of the assignment; select a topic which not only interests you but one with which you have a comfortable level of familiarity and competence.

Something Old, Something New

In every course, there are always "classic" term paper topics. These are perpetually valid topics which are typically based on one of the core foundations of the subject.

Ready examples include *The Civil War, Dante's Inferno*

and *Einstein's Theory of Relativity.*

Teachers cannot easily ban such term paper topics, but they can harbor a secret boredom with having to read them term after term after term.

Because they are classic topics, they do have an on-going value to each succeeding generation of students. (That's why they're classics!)

There is a way, however, of taking such a classic topic and updating it in terms of more current developments and events.

We are not proposing any specific topics; we are simply showing you the possibilities of employing this creative, contemporary approach in selecting an "old" topic and giving it a new perspective.

With that caveat, consider these possibilities:

The Civil War could become *Was The Korean War A 'Civil War' Which America Should Never Have Entered?*

Dante's Inferno could become *Is Dante's Inferno One of Today's Fundamental Evangelical Themes?*

Einstein's Theory of Relativity could easily be updated as *Recent Challenges To Einstein's Theory of Relativity.*

Length, Time and Specific Instructions

Virtually every term paper assignment will include a minimum or maximum length, a specific due date for submission and whatever other instructions the teacher issues with regard to the execution and fulfillment of the assignment.

Each of these factors will obviously play a critical role in determining your topic.

If you have a 2,500 word limit and two weeks notice, your paper will have to be no less complete but it will have to be relatively modest both in length and in scope.

If you have a 10,000 word limit and six weeks notice, you will be expected to produce a significantly more profound paper.

An accepted "rule of thumb" is that a double-spaced typewritten page contains approximately 250 words.

Teachers will not be pleased if you fail to work within the parameters of the assignment.

Similarly, you will be expected to adhere to whatever other instructions accompany the assignment.

Keep in mind that a term paper is not the proper forum for breaking (or even bending) rules.

When In Doubt, Ask!

If teachers could select a universal bumper sticker to attach to their cars, it would probably say *Talk To Me!*

Most teachers are willing, even eager, to hear from their students, particularly when it comes to discussing such challenging assignments as a term paper.

So, never be afraid to discuss your paper with your teacher in advance of writing it; he or she will be flattered at your commitment to produce a solid paper and you will be relieved to learn that you are on, or have been directed to, the right track.

CHAPTER

3

A QUESTION OF STYLE

It's no accident that this is the shortest chapter in the book.

After all of the planning, preparation and research, eventually a term paper has to be written.

Writing, like fashion, comes in a variety of styles.

Outside of the school environment, we tend to accept certain clichés about writing: Doctors' prescriptions are always illegible, lawyers will always write a page when a paragraph would do, etc.

Students faced with a term paper often believe that they have to abandon their everyday vocabulary and writing style in the presentation of their paper.

This is an inaccurate, and potentially damaging, belief.

It is true, of course, that some of the elements of a term paper are formal and unvarying. As you will discover, footnotes and bibliographies fall into this category of scholarly formality.

Correct grammar, spelling and usage have to be maintained throughout a term paper, as well.

The style and presentation of the paper, however, are very personal and subjective matters.

Your paper has to be clear, comprehensive and convincing in order to be successful.

The most effective way of achieving this is to "be yourself."

Complex ideas are often most effectively established by the use of simple, declarative sentences.

Many of these sentences can stand by themselves as paragraphs, depending on the completeness of their content.

A term paper paragraph does not have to look like a page of the *Internal Revenue Code*, which often goes on for hundreds of lines without a grammatical break.

Most likely, you are distrustful of pretentious people.

Similarly, teachers are frequently distrustful of pretentious writing, troubled by the notion that "five dollar words" are masking incomplete thoughts in a student's attempt to hide behind lazy impressions rather than original expressions.

So, don't give into the discredited belief that an excessive presentation will provide your term paper with an advantage.

In fact, the opposite is more likely: *An overwritten paper will frequently produce an underwhelming grade.*

CHAPTER

4

GETTING STARTED, GETTING ORGANIZED

Many of us share the common tendency to put off until tomorrow what we should have done yesterday. Typically, our procrastination will produce last-minute results which are inevitably less satisfactory than those which we would have achieved had we been more thoughtful about our management of time.

Putting off a term paper will produce a similar outcome.

Teachers, like Internal Revenue Service examiners, are skilled at spotting hasty, last-minute submissions.

Taxpayers can usually atone for their haste with payments of penalties and interest coupled with stern warnings not to treat their obligations so casually in the future.

Students are not so fortunate. What the teacher receives will determine the grade you receive, and not even well-intentioned promises of future diligence will succeed in modifying the consequences of present negligence.

The Sooner, The Better!

Unlike overnight homework or reading assignments, term papers can be deceptive from a scheduling perspective.

A frequent reaction to a term paper assignment whose due date is weeks away is, "I've got plenty of time."

That reaction is usually followed by, "I can't believe it's *already* due on Monday!"

Comparing an overnight reading assignment to a term paper is like comparing a 50-yard dash to a 26-mile marathon.

Even if you're out of shape, you can probably make a respectable (if not winning) showing in a short race. Competing in a marathon, however, demands training, conditioning and an entirely different mind set. If you're out of shape for a marathon, you'll never even get close to the finish line.

In academic terms, a term paper is similar to a marathon.

Thus, to properly prepare for the challenge of a term paper, you should begin the process of dealing with your assignment within 24 hours of receiving it.

Our acronym for this process is PASS.

That's easy to remember because, after all, to PASS is the primary objective of every term paper.

What may slightly surprise you is what PASS represents:

P — Ponder
A — Attack
S — Sit
S — Submit

Ponder

A term paper offers the creative student a kaleidoscope of possibilities.

The subject matter can be approached from a variety of angles. The selection of sources and resources offers similar choices. And then, most uniquely of all (without making the impossible decision of reinventing the wheel), the creative student will want to put his own perspective on the paper.

All of these considerations, critical to the success or failure of the paper, take time.

This first step in the PASS process is not dissimilar to free association, where you simply let your mind wander (and ponder) through the options which are open to you.

You don't have to make any final decisions at this point; rather, you ought to begin to get excited about the paper and to begin to develop your approach to researching and writing it.

The only hard decision you should make is to set (and determine to stick to!) a schedule, allowing yourself enough time to produce a paper of the quality and quantity which your teacher expects.

This pondering process may sound almost too easy to be useful.

In fact, it will set the tone for the balance of your assignment; it is, in the most meaningful sense of the expression, "quality time."

It is an advantage which you should make every effort not to deny yourself.

Attack

Once you've made some hard decisions, such as the approach you will take in the presentation of your paper and the materials you will use in support of that approach, you've got to get down to the hard work of research and the even more difficult process of writing your first draft.

Future chapters will deal with many of the details and specifics which you must utilize, such as outlining, note-taking, writing your first draft, foot-noting, and the preparation of your bibliography. This early chapter is simply designed to condition you for the impending task.

Attack is not too strong a word; one definition of the word, according to the *American Heritage Dictionary,* is "to start work with vigor."

A winning term paper demands commitment and vigor.

Following the luxury of pondering, now you must deploy the energy of attacking your project with dedication, determination and desire.

Sit

We mean this literally.

You should set your paper aside, and work on other matters, other assignments, other things.

In terms of your paper, it should sit and you should sit.

After the intensity of producing the first draft, you need some time and distance away from one another.

This "holiday" shouldn't be excessive; perhaps a day or three at the most.

This "holiday" can only be taken once you have worked

your way through the term paper process as it is discussed and defined in the next seven chapters. It is noted here simply because "sitting" is an integral component of PASS.

You will be surprised by what you read when you return to the paper, and you will be in a much more objective position to improve and edit the paper than you would have been immediately after finishing your concluding paragraph.

The emotional drain of researching and writing will have somewhat dissolved, and you will be able to put together a final, revised version with much less stress.

Procrastination will deny you this part of the process, which can often make the different between an ordinary term paper and an extraordinary one.

So, as if you didn't have enough reasons not to procrastinate, you can add this critical advantage to your list, as well.

Submit

You've done all you can; now comes the moment of truth.

The only thought which we would add here is that neatness *does* count.

Teachers, who are only human, will regard a neat, clean and organized paper with favor. It makes their task easier, and it reflects the work of a competent and considerate student. It also avoids any suggestion of last-minute maneuvering, as if your last page came out of your typewriter or word processor moments before you entered the classroom.

With any luck, PASS will help you to live up to its acronym!

CHAPTER

5

HOW TO USE THE LIBRARY

Like the color of ink on paper, many students' feelings about the library are either black or white.

Those who love the library may remember happy Saturday mornings spent in the children's section listening to a passionate librarian spinning magical fairy tales.

Those who dislike, or even fear, the library may recall images of stern-faced librarians telling them to sit down, be quiet and not disturb anyone or anything in their intimidating setting.

Hopefully, you have positive feelings about the library. Even if that's not the case, you're going to have to learn to use the library efficiently.

Trying to write a term paper without taking advantage of the library's resources is like trying to ride a bicycle with two flat tires: *You may be able to get from here to there but it's going to be a rough ride.*

How Many Kinds of Libraries Are There?

We've been speaking of *the* library as if there were only one. Obviously, that's not the case. The reason we've been using the singular is because that's the way most of us refer to libraries, expecting those to whom we're speaking to know *the* library we have in mind.

When a mother asks a child whether or not he's going to the library, both of them understand that she has the local branch of the community's public library in mind.

Similarly, when a college student announces that the library is his destination, he doesn't have to specify that he has the college library in mind.

These examples suggest that libraries are often a natural point of reference in our lives, logistically as well as literally.

In fact, there are three-and-a-half different kinds of libraries:

Public libraries. Most communities, even the smallest of towns, have at least one public library. It is the first library most of us visit and, depending on its size and resources, it can be a library that becomes increasingly useful as our educational needs and intellectual curiosity expand.

High school libraries. This is our "half" category because we cannot include high school libraries in the same category as college and university libraries. High school libraries (sometimes called "media centers") are generally modest but useful, because their collections often relate directly to the school curriculum.

College and university libraries. Depending on the size, financial strength and reputation of the institution, their resources vary. Typically, however, these libraries are well-stocked treasure troves of information, responsive to student needs and invaluable in the preparation of term papers. High school students will often be permitted to use these libraries. However, they will not usually have the ability to borrow any materials.

Special libraries. These are libraries established by other institutions, such as museums or trade associations or corporations. They tend to be specific rather than general, directly related to the interest or business of the sponsoring institution — but they frequently contain materials and information not available elsewhere.

As we observed at the beginning of this section, there is no such place as *the* library. On the other hand, the only library in the United States which doesn't fall within any of our three-and-a-half categories could properly be characterized as *the* nation's library.

The Library of Congress, in Washington, D.C., is a unique and all encompassing institution, containing millions of books and priceless documents available no where else in the country, or the world. It is a haven for scholars and the repository of much of the nation's knowledge.

Your First Stop: The Information Desk

Like fingerprints and snowflakes, no two libraries are exactly alike.

What virtually all libraries do have in common is an information desk under the supervision of a librarian who can make your life infinitely easier. All you have to do is ask; information desk librarians are in the full-time business of providing answers.

The information desk will enable you to quickly become familiar with the layout and resources of the library and to conserve significant amounts of time and energy locating the materials which you need.

Some libraries have directories and maps available; some college and university libraries schedule tours for entering freshman; all libraries will help you to understand and utilize them with maximum efficiency and effectiveness.

You will want to know such matters as the location of the reference room, where periodicals are kept and how (whether as actual copies or on microfilm), and whether or not there is more than one central card catalog.

Next to the information desk librarian, the library's card catalog will become your most useful compass.

Therefore, the card catalog merits its own section.

The Card Catalog

Whoever created the slogan "Let your fingers do the walking" for the Yellow Pages must have spent a great deal of time in libraries.

The slogan could apply just as directly to every library's card catalog.

The card catalog is the complete directory of all of the library's available materials. To use the card catalog, you will have to know at least one element of the publication you are seeking: either its author, its title or its subject.

Each publication is listed at least three times in the card catalog:

(1) By author, with his last name listed first.

(2) By title, beginning with the first word (other than *A*, *An* or *The*).

(3) By subject, with several cards listed if the publication deals with more than a single subject.

We have provided a sample of each type of card:

AUTHOR'S CARD

362.6
CRYST Crystal, Stephen, 1946 -
America's old age crisis : public policy and the two worlds of aging / Stephen Crystal. — New York : Basic Books, c1982.
p. cm.
Includes bibliographical references and index.

1. Aged — Government policy — United States. 2. Aged — Service for — United States. 3. Aged — United States — Family relationships. 4. Social security — United States. I. Title

TITLE CARD

America's old age crisis

362.6
CRYST Crystal, Stephen, 1946 -
America's old age crisis : public policy and the two worlds of aging / Stephen Crystal. — New York : Basic Books, c1982.
p. cm.
Includes bibliographical references and index.

1. Aged — Government policy — United States. 2. Aged — Service for — United States. 3. Aged — United States — Family relationships. 4. Social security — United States. I. Title

SUBJECT CARD

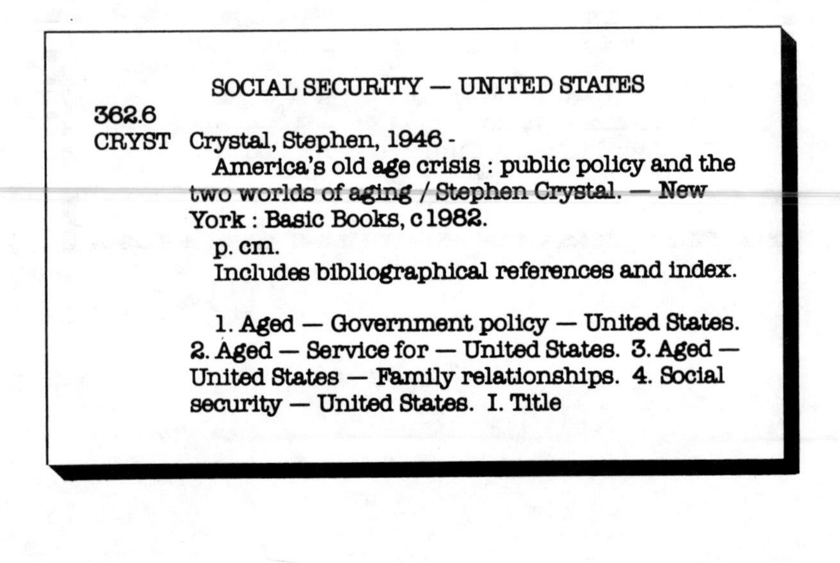

SOCIAL SECURITY — UNITED STATES

362.6
CRYST Crystal, Stephen, 1946 -
America's old age crisis : public policy and the two worlds of aging / Stephen Crystal. — New York : Basic Books, c1982.
p. cm.
Includes bibliographical references and index.

1. Aged — Government policy — United States. 2. Aged — Service for — United States. 3. Aged — United States — Family relationships. 4. Social security — United States. I. Title

The specific location of the publication which you are seeking will be indicated by a sequence of numbers in the upper left hand corner of each entry card.

That number has been determined by the Dewey Decimal System, which has been the primary method of classifying library books for over one hundred years.

The Dewey Decimal System

The Dewey Decimal System divides all of the publications contained within the library into ten main classes:

000 - 099	General Works (Encylopedias, etc.)
100 - 199	Philosophy and Related Subjects
200 - 299	Religion
300 - 399	Social Sciences
400 - 499	Language
500 - 599	Pure Science
600 - 699	Applied Science and Technology
700 - 799	The Arts
800 - 899	Literature
900 - 999	History

Each class is further divided into ten divisions. Using History as an example, it is divided into these ten divisions:

900 - 909	General World History
910 - 919	Geography and Travel
920 - 929	Biography
930 - 939	Ancient Civilizations
940 - 949	General European History

950 - 959 General Asian History
960 - 969 Africa
970 - 979 North America
980 - 989 South America
990 - 999 The Rest of the World

Finally, each division is divided further into ten sections. Using General European History as an example, it is divided into these ten sections:

940 General European History
941 Great Britain
942 Great Britain (continued)
943 Germany and Eastern Europe
944 France
945 Italy
946 Spain and Portugal
947 Soviet Union
948 Scandinavia
949 Other European Countries

Thus, the first three numbers in the Dewey Decimal System represent the main class, its division and its section. The decimal in the Dewey Decimal System is placed after each three-digit number, enabling the classifications to become very specific. For example:

940 - General European History
940.1 - Middle Ages
940.2 - Modern Europe

These further subdivisions can be extended even further. For example:

940.51 - World War II

The Dewey Decimal System is the primary library classification system.

The Library of Congress, because of the magnitude of its collection, had to devise its own system of classification. Its system uses letters to divide the areas of knowledge into twenty categories (in place of Dewey's ten main classes). Only the Library of Congress and a few enormous libraries use this alternative system.

The Library Can "Reach Out" For You

Virtually all libraries have the ability to borrow books and periodicals from other libraries. This "interlibrary loan" agreement enables you to gain access to materials which your library doesn't own. However, this can be a time-consuming process which should be started well in advance of your deadline.

More and more libraries have the ability to conduct "on-line" computer searches, to locate additional sources of reference for your term paper from existing data bases of information. They will charge for this service. The rate will vary based on the time expended, the telephone charges, and the fees charged by the data base network.

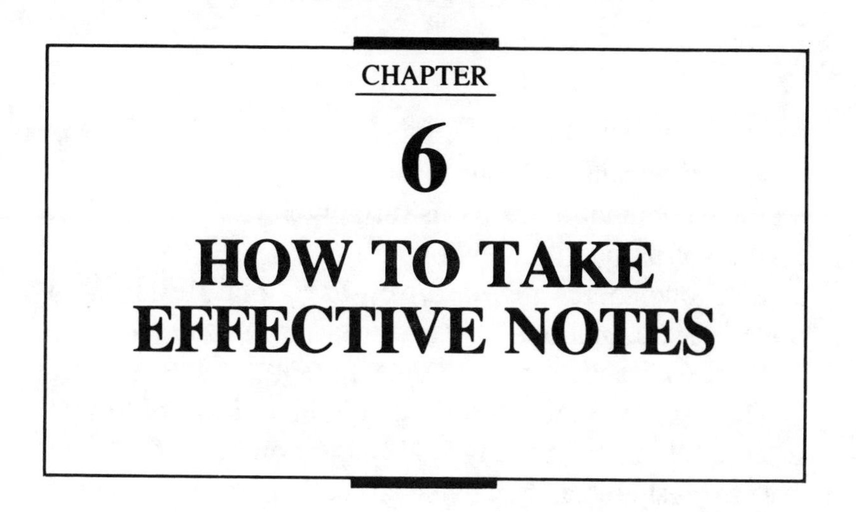

CHAPTER 6
HOW TO TAKE EFFECTIVE NOTES

The truth is that if, for one reason or another, you fail to take notes in an important class, you can make up for the lapse by borrowing a classmate's notes.

If, however, you fail to take complete and accurate notes in the process of researching your term paper, you will not get a second chance.

You're on your own in the preparation of a term paper — each student's paper is unique — and the only "insurance" you can obtain is your own sense of caution and completeness.

By the time you sit down to write your paper, surrounded by your notes and filled with the impressions of hundreds of pages of independent reading and research, you will be far away from the library and the source material of the notes which will form the basis of your paper.

Must You Use Index Cards?

There is essentially universal agreement among students and teachers that index cards (usually 3 x 5) are the ideal format for preparing a bibliography.

With one source per card, you have total flexibility in updating your bibliography as you add and subtract titles to or from your collection of source material.

The conventional wisdom extends this index card format to note-taking, with the typical suggestion being that your note cards should be somewhat larger (perhaps 5 x 8). There are two reasons for this: (1) you will be able to easily distinguish your note cards from your bibliography cards and (2) for notes as well as the bibliography, the index card system will provide you with maximum flexibility.

Some students, however, find the index card format uncomfortable.

While they have little problem adapting to index cards for their bibliography, they cannot accommodate themselves to this format for the purpose of note-taking.

Our response is simple: *use whatever format works for you.*

It may be a pocket pad or a loose-leaf book or even (in this age of technology) a pocket recorder or a portable lap-top computer.

The majority of term papers *are* prepared using index cards, and our suggestions for effective note-taking are presented for this traditional, time-tested format.

Just as we wouldn't presume to tell you whether to use a ball point pen, a No. 2 pencil or a quill for your notes, we wouldn't presume to suggest that the art of note-taking is an absolute one.

However, no matter which system you employ, you will have to record the same basic information.

How Many Sides of the Card Should You Use?

Again, there is essentially universal agreement that, if you are using index cards for your notes, you should only include one idea per card.

The controversy arises between those who believe that each card should be only used on one side and those who believe that writing on both sides is more efficient.

In this instance, we do have a personal preference — and it comes down on the side of the traditionalists: one side per card seems to work better.

Two Pieces of Data Which All Cards Must Include

All note cards must have a subject heading, either on the top line or in the upper left-hand corner. You must be able to determine almost instantly what each card is about.

All note cards must also include the source information which will become part of your bibliography. This means that each word must clearly identify the source of the material on that card.

When you create several cards of notes from a single source, the first card must contain the complete bibliographic information: author, title, publishing data. For subsequent cards from that same source, you can devise a personal shorthand system for identifying the source without repeating all of the data.

Whether your shorthand system uses letters, numbers or symbols, it must be clear and unambiquous.

We believe letters are the easiest to use. Therefore, we are using the letter A for our examples. The page numbers beneath refer to the pages within the book from which the transcribed material was taken.

Teachers are unforgiving when information is ascribed to an incorrect source.

This is a sample of a bibliography card:

A

Crystal, Stephen
America's Old Age Crisis
New York : Basic Books, 1982

Quotation Cards

When you are taking a direct quotation from a source, be very careful to faithfully transcribe it to your note card.

If you are omitting some words, you can indicate that

with three dots contained with an ellipse, like this: (. . .).

If you are adding some words of your own to the quotation, you can indicate that by including your words within brackets, like this: **[in my opinion]**.

These are samples of each type of quotation card:

DIRECT QUOTATION

A

p. 192

"The flow of resources to the older generation is there and will continue to be there. In managing it, however, we can and should do better."

DIRECT QUOTATION WITH OMISSIONS

A

p. 9

"A vast host of agencies . . . makes up the 'aging network'."

QUOTATION WITH YOUR OPINION

A

p. 192

[I agree with Mr. Crystal's belief that]
"the flow of resources to the older generation is there and will continue to be there. In managing it, however, we can and should do better."

Paraphrase Cards

Even if you are not using a source's exact words, you will have to credit that source for the essence of the idea which you are presenting.

Since you will not be using quotation marks, make certain that your version is distinctly different from the original quotation. Otherwise, you can unconsciously find yourself in the awkward position of having unintentionally plagiarized someone else's proprietary material.

Plagiarism is defined as using another's ideas without crediting them. It is a serious offense even if it unintentional.

A paraphrase card might look like this:

PARAPHRASE

A

p. 3

Crystal believes there is insufficient understanding of existing programs for the care and support of the aging.

Summary, or Commentary, Cards

These cards will summarize a related body of information in your own words.

Typically, they will consist of a combination of material from the source together with your own observations.

Again, you will have to be careful to clearly distinguish your personal commentary from the information which you are summarizing.

Most plagiarism (which is a school's version of treason or a capital offense) is unintentional, often unconscious, the product of the research superimposing itself upon the paper without — as the adage goes — any malice aforethought on the part of the student.

The consequences for plagiarism, however, can be severe, often leading to expulsion or suspension. Therefore, we must again remind you that each student has an obligation to exercise extreme caution in this regard.

This is a sample summary card:

A

p. 192

"America's old age crisis" — unlike many other political and social issues — affects all of us.

By the time we reach "old age," there will hopefully no longer be an "old age crisis."

When you sit down to write your paper, your note cards will form the basis of your composition. Thus, you will be at a great disadvantage if they are not clear and comprehensive.

Many students carry a set of index cards with them at all times during the term paper process, in the belief that sources can emerge in the unlikeliest places at the most unexpected times.

Even if the premise doesn't work, the cards will serve as a constant reminder of your assignment, like a silent but constant alarm.

CHAPTER

7

HOW TO PREPARE A BIBLIOGRAPHY

As you're taking notes, you should also be developing a preliminary, or working, bibliography.

A bibliography is a listing of all of the information sources which you used in support of your paper. It includes both book and non-book sources.

Typically, your preliminary bibliography will be much longer than your final bibliography. At first, you will gather (and create bibliography cards for) a wide selection of material. Ultimately, you will eliminate some of these potential sources. Since the bibliography attached to your term paper will only include those sources which you actually used, it will in all likelihood be shorter than your working bibliography.

Your Bibliography Card

Our suggested format for creating a bibliography is to put each source on a separate 3 x 5 index card. This will enable you to easily keep your working bibliography current as you add and delete titles.

Each card must contain this information:

(1) The author's name, last name first.

(2) The title of the material.

(3) The publication data: place of publication, publisher and copyright date.

Your bibliography is placed at the end of your term paper, and all of the sources are listed in alphabetical order by the author's last name. Where there is no author, then the first word of the title is used (disregarding *a, an* and *the).*

On the bibliography page, the author's last name is placed flush with the left-hand margin of the paper and all subsequent lines for that entry are indented five spaces.

The following examples of bibliographic entries for all types of information sources and a sample bibliography page have been furnished by the Media Services Department of the Greenwich (CT) Public Schools. Greenwich High School, each of whose students are provided with these examples, is consistently ranked as one of the top ten public high schools in the United States.

Examples of Bibliographic Citations

Book with a SINGLE AUTHOR

Stauffer, Donald Barlow. *A Short History of American Poetry.* New York: E.P. Dutton, 1974.

Book with an EDITOR instead of an author

Gibson, James, ed. *The Complete Poems of Thomas Hardy.* New York: Macmillan, 1976.

Book with TWO AUTHORS

Link, Arthur S., and William B. Catton. *American Epoch: A History of the United States Since 1890.* New York: Knopf, 1963.

Book with THREE AUTHORS

Adams, William, Peter Cohn, and Barry Slepian. *Afro-American Literature: Drama:* Boston: Houghton Mifflin, 1970.

Book with FOUR or MORE AUTHORS

Goldner, Orville, et al. *The Making of King Kong.* New York: Ballantine, 1975.

Book with CORPORATE AUTHOR

United Nations. *Statistical Yearbook, 1978.* New York: United Nations, 1979.

Book with NO KNOWN AUTHOR

Literary Market Place: The Directory of American Book Publishing. 1976-77 ed. New York: Bowker, 1976.

Book translated from a FOREIGN LANGUAGE

Solzhenitsyn, Aleksandr I. *The First Circle.* Trans. Thomas P. Whitney. New York: Harper & Row, 1968.

ONE VOLUME of a work in SEVERAL VOLUMES

Sullivan, Mark. *Over Here: 1914-1918.* Vol. V. of *Our Times.* New York: Scribner, 1972.

Work in a COLLECTION by DIFFERENT AUTHORS

Lisca, Peter. "The Grapes of Wrath: In *Steinbeck: A Collection of Critical Essays.* Ed. Robert Murray Davis. Englewood Cliffs, N.J.: Prentice-Hall, 1972.

Work in a COLLECTION by the SAME AUTHOR

Williams, Tennessee. "Summer and Smoke." In *Four Plays.* New York: New American Library, 1976.

GOVERNMENT PUBLICATION

U.S. Dept. of Agriculture. *Yearbook of Agriculture, 1974: Shopper's Guide.* 93rd Cong., 2nd sess. H. Doc. 93-279. Washington, D.C.: GPO, 1975.

PAMPHLET

Chronicle Guidance Publications, Inc. *Cartoonists: Occupational Brief.* 4th ed. D.O.T. 141. Moravia, N.Y.: CGP, 1978.

Article in an ENCYCLOPEDIA — SIGNED

"Cells." *The New Book of Popular Science.* (1979).

Article in a PERIODICAL — WEEKLY

Stone, Martin. "Energy Jigsaw Puzzle." *U.S. News,* 27 Aug. 1979, p. 76.

Article in a PERIODICAL — MONTHLY

Bugialli, George. "Share a Rustic Italian Christmas Eve." *House and Garden,* Dec. 1978, pp. 140-143.

Article in a WEEKLY PERIODICAL with volume and number given

"AFL-CIO Looks at Economy." *Facts on File,* 40, No 1051, 29 Feb. 1980, p. 146.

Article in a NEWSPAPER

Brody, Jane E. "Nutritional Standards for the 80's." *New York Times,* City Ed., 19 March 1980, Sec. C, p.1, cols. 5-6.

> If the article is unsigned, start citation with title, "Nutritional Standards . . ."

LETTER TO THE EDITOR

Crummett, Warren B. Letter. *Science,* 107 (1980), 148.

REVIEW

Hartung, Phillip T. "The Screen." Rev. of *2001: A Space Odyssey,* by Stanley Kubrick. *Commonweal,* 3 May 1968, pp. 207-208.

> If the review is unsigned, begin the citation with the title of the review or, if untitled, simply with "Rev. of . . ." which stands for review of.

Telephone INTERVIEW

Yanklevich, Tatyana. Telephone interview. 20 Feb. 1980.

Personal INTERVIEW

Jones, Jane. Personal interview in the Museum of Modern Art. 21 Jan. 1980.

Sound FILMSTRIP with an AUTHOR

McDaniel, Marion and Michael McDaniel. *Redesigning Man: Science and Human Values* (Filmstrip). New York: Harper & Row Media Program, 1974, 6 rolls, col., with 6 cassettes.

Sound FILMSTRIP with NO AUTHOR

"Robert Frost" (Filmstrip). In *The American Experience in Literature: Poets of the 20th Century*. Chicago: Encyclopedia Britannica Educ. Corp., 1964, 5 rolls, col., with 5 cassettes.

ART PRINT

Monet, Claude. *Boats at Argenteuil* (Print). U.S.A.: Shorewood Press, Inc., n.d., col., 16½ x 25 in.

SLIDE

Surrealism (Slide). Stamford, Ct.: Educational Dimensions, 1974, 20 slides, col., 2 x 2 in.

MICROFORM

"Watch Out for Food Poisoning" (Microfilm). *Changing Times*. Aug. 1975, pp. 36-38.

MOTION PICTURE

The Food Revolution (Motion Picture). New York: McGraw-Hill, 1968, 17 min., sd., col., 16 mm.

Sound RECORDING or CASSETTE

Whitman, Walt. *Leaves of Grass* (Sound Recording). Ed Begley, reader. Caedmon, n.d., disc TC 1037.

VIDEO TAPE or VIDEOCASSETTE

Wolfe, Pamela. "Pam Wolfe Bakes Bread" (Videorecording). Presented at Greenwich High School, 1977, cassette, 30 min., b & w, 3/4 in.

SAMPLE BIBLIOGRAPHY PAGE

Arentzen, E.D. "Oceanographic Submersibles." *McGraw-Hill Encyclopedia of Science and Technology.* (1971).

Brody, Jane E. "Nutritional Standard for the 80's." *New York Times,* City Ed., 19 March 1980, Sec. C, p. 1, cols. 5-6.

"Cells." *The New Book of Popular Science.* (1979).

Crummett, Warren B. Letter. *Science,* 107 (1980), 148.

The Food Revolution (Motion Picture). New York: McGraw-Hill, 1968, 17 min., sd., col., 16 mm.

Gibson, James, ed. *The Complete Poems of Thomas Hardy.* New York: Macmillan, 1976.

Madison, Arthur. American Global Democracy, 1800 to 1950. New York: Watts, 1977.

----------. *Vandalism: The Not-So-Senseless Crime.* New York: Seabury Press, 1970.

> Use this form when citing another book by the same author.

Stone, Martin. "Energy Jigsaw Puzzle." *U.S. News,* 17 Aug. 1979, p. 76.

United Nations. *Statistical Yearbook, 1978.* New York: United Nations, 1979.

U.S. Dept. of Agriculture. *Yearbook of Agriculture, 1974: Shopper's Guide.* 93rd Cong., 2nd sess. H. Doc. 93-279. Washington, D.C.: GPO, 1975.

CHAPTER

8

PREPARING YOUR OUTLINE

Preparing the outline of, and for, your term paper is similar to exercising: It can be tedious but you'll be in much better condition for having made the effort.

An outline is the interim step between the completion of your initial research and the writing of your first draft.

The preparation of the outline is really engaging in the process of discovery because, in fact, as you develop your outline you will learn a great deal about the nature (and strength or weakness) of your paper:

(1) First, of course, it will force you to organize your thoughts in a comprehensive and logical sequence.

(2) Second, it will test the validity of your central theme, or thesis.

(3) Third, as you arrange your material, it will reveal any gaps in your presentation, missing pieces of data which you will need to include to justify your premise and conclusion.

Because of its skeletal nature, an outline forces you to

deal with the basic flow and structure of your paper.

If it feels right, then you are well on your way towards producing a winning term paper.

If it reveals flaws or lapses, you will still be in good shape because you will have found them in time to correct them.

Our two sample outlines follow the most common and familiar format of the majority of term paper outlines.

Our first example is what is called a **topic outline.**

Our second example, expanding on the same material, is called a **sentence outline.**

Many teachers suggest proceeding from one to the other, with the third and final step in the evolution being the term paper itself.

Thus the recommended sequence is:

Topic Outline ➞ Sentence Outline ➞ Term Paper.

Topic Outline

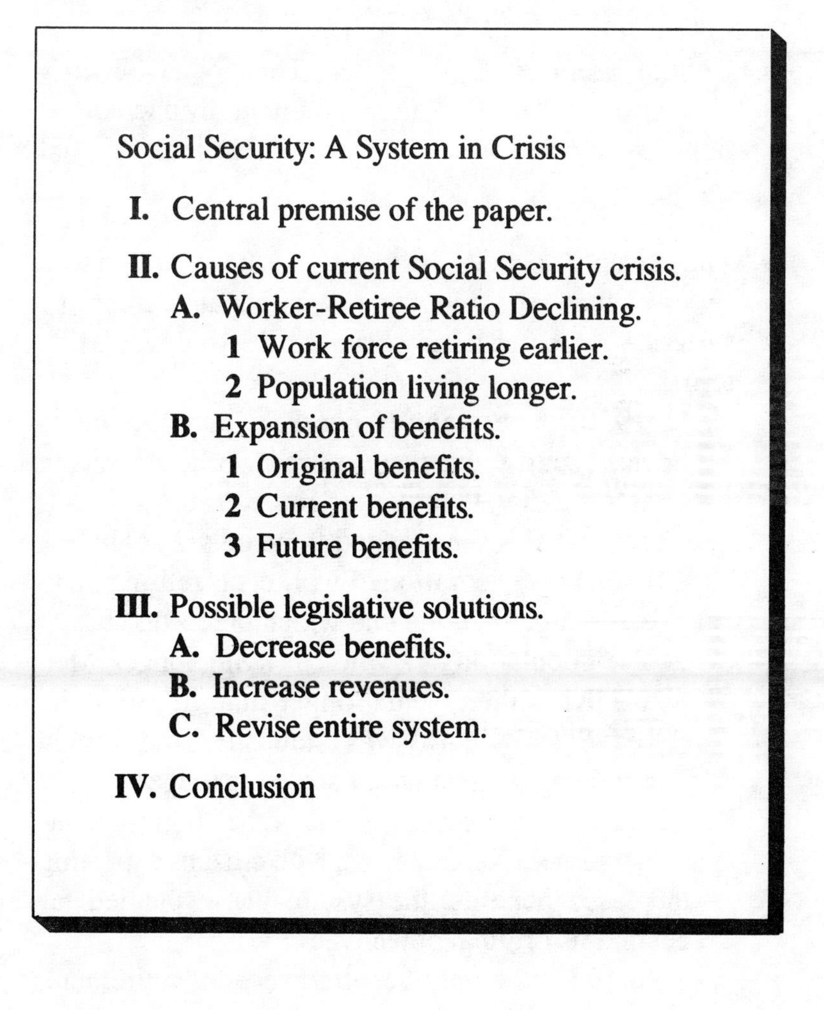
Social Security: A System in Crisis

I. Central premise of the paper.

II. Causes of current Social Security crisis.
  A. Worker-Retiree Ratio Declining.
    1 Work force retiring earlier.
    2 Population living longer.
  B. Expansion of benefits.
    1 Original benefits.
    2 Current benefits.
    3 Future benefits.

III. Possible legislative solutions.
  A. Decrease benefits.
  B. Increase revenues.
  C. Revise entire system.

IV. Conclusion

Sentence Outline

Social Security: A System in Crisis

I. Central premise of the paper: The Social Security System, created in 1935 and fundamentally unchanged since, must be revised if it is to survive into the next century.

II. The current Social Security crisis has been caused by a series of factors which was not anticipated when the system was created during Franklin D. Roosevelt's first term.

   A. In 1950, there were 16 workers contributing to Social Security for every retired worker receiving benefits; today, that worker-retiree ratio is 3-to-1, and by 2027 it is estimated to be only 2-to-1.

      1 Each new generation of workers is retiring at an earlier age than the one which preceeded it.

      2 The population as a whole is living longer. Men are living three years longer than in 1935, the year Social Security was established, and women are living an average of six years longer.

   B. Because Social Security is one of the "hottest" constituent issues for Congress, with citizens expecting increased benefits, the system has expanded far beyond its original objectives.

      1 In 1935, the only benefits were for retirement, death and disability.

      2 Current benefits, including Medicare, have pushed the system to the edge of insolvency.

3 Prospective pending benefits, notably the possibility of National Health Insurance, threaten to accelerate Social Security's fiscal weakness.

III. The 1983 revisions to Social Security only provided short-term relief; therefore, a reluctant Congress will have to grapple with this controversial and complicated issue in the very near future in order to secure its long-term survival.

A. The entire schedule of benefits will have to be reviewed and revised in view of the changing demographics of the workplace.

B. Revenues into the system will have to be increased, despite Congress' fear of severe constituent backlash to such measures.

C. While (A) and (B) deal with changes to the current system, it may be necessary to scrap the original fundamentals of the existing system and create one designed for the new realities of the new century.

IV. Social Security is a system in crisis and only a Congressional response of equal urgency can save the system and provide security to Americans in the 21st century equivalent to the protection and benefits which their parents and grandparents received during the previous 65 years.

CHAPTER

9

WHAT SHOULD GO INTO YOUR FIRST DRAFT

To this point, you have invested considerable time and energy in the development of your term paper.

You have one more major investment left: your first draft.

Writing the first draft, however, offers you some surprising opportunities for fun.

Imagine that we added a question mark to the title of this chapter: *What should go into your first draft?*

The answer is fun all by itself: *Everything . . . including the kitchen sink!*

We're not suggesting that all of the discipline which you have brought to the research process should now be abandoned as you begin to write the paper; rather, we're suggesting that your first draft is the place to flex all of the mental muscles which you've worked so hard.

The products of that hard work — your note cards and

your bibliography cards — should be close at hand as you begin your first draft.

The note cards should be arranged in a logical order following the sequence of your outline.

The bibliography cards should be arranged alphabetically.

You may want to have some other potentially helpful guides on hand, such as a dictionary and a thesaurus.

Like the lead paragraph of a newspaper story, your opening paragraph has to command attention. It sets forth the central premise of your paper, and it should do so in a confident and compelling manner.

If that opening paragraph doesn't come easily, you can move beyond it for the time being. Our thought, however, would be to try to write at least a tentative version. The opening is critical and establishes a mood and purpose for the paper; moving forward without it will create a vacuum.

As you move ahead, essentially following the order of the outline from your note cards (which are now flowering into a harvest of thoughts), you should not worry about editing yourself.

It will be much easier to delete material from a paper which is too long than to add material to one which falls short of the teacher's requirements. (This is the thought which prompted our comment about the kitchen sink.)

You should pay attention to the logical flow of the paper, and to the strength and direction of the paper as it moves from the opening premise to the closing summary.

Like a lawyer's summation, your closing paragraph is also one of the most critical sections of the paper. It will be your “last word” before your teacher has the (ultimate) “last word!”

When you sat down to write your first draft you were in the midst of critical phase two of the four phases of the **PASS** process which we introduced in chapter three.

P — Ponder.
A — Attack.
S — Sit.
S — Submit.

Now that your first draft is finished, you have completed the first half of the **PASS** process.

You have pondered and prepared.

You have attacked all aspects of the thesis.

Now, as we suggested in chapter three, it’s time for you and your paper to “sit” before you write and submit your final draft. Simply distract yourself for a while before returning to the paper for the last time.

You’ve earned it and, by taking this break, you may even earn a higher grade, as well.

CHAPTER

10

PROPER USE OF FOOTNOTES

Traditionally, scholars have credited all sources from which they have derived information or ideas. Term papers, which are in the scholarly tradition, maintain this honor system of documentation — of giving credit where credit is due.

We have already discussed the bibliography, which acknowledges all of the sources used in the preparation of the term paper.

The other form of documentation is the subject of this chapter: footnotes.

You should use a footnote when you are directly quoting an author's words, when you refer to someone else's idea or opinion (even though you are doing so indirectly), and when you are using information taken from a specific source (including statistics, figures, definitions, illustrations, charts or graphs).

Well-known facts, broadly defined as "common knowledge," do not have to be acknowledged in footnotes.

Footnotes are usually numbered consecutively throughout the paper. They can also be numbered separately for each page, with the footnotes on each page beginning with "1." The preferred method is to number footnotes consecutively.

Footnotes can be placed at the bottom (foot) of the page or, as shown in the sample, at the end of your paper, preceeding the bibliography. (Technically, when they are placed at the end of the paper, they are considered to be endnotes rather than footnotes.)

In the context of the paper, the number of the footnote is placed *after* the quote or citation. For example, your paper would look like this:

"With few exceptions, Faulkner's best early stories are those in which he wrote of his own region."[1]

In the footnote, however, this number is placed at the *beginning* of the footnote. For example, your footnote would look like this:

---

[1]Arthur Voss, *The American Short Story: A Critical Survey* (Norman: Univ. of Oklahoma Press, 1973), p. 246.

EXAMPLES OF FOOTNOTES

Book with a SINGLE AUTHOR

[1]Donald Barlow Stauffer, *A Short History of American Poetry* (New York: E.P. Dutton, 1974), p. 173.

Book with an EDITOR instead of an author

[2]James Gibson, ed., *The Complete Poems of Thomas Hardy* (New York: Macmillan, 1976), p. 786.

Book with TWO AUTHORS

[3]Arthur S. Link and William B. Catton, *American Epoch: A History of the United States Since 1890* (New York, Knopf, 1963), p. 502.

Book with THREE AUTHORS

[4]William Adams, Peter Cohn, and Barry Slepian, *Afro-American Literature: Drama* (Boston: Houghton Mifflin, 1970), p. 9.

Book with FOUR or MORE AUTHORS

[5]Orville Goldner, et al., *The Making of King Kong* (New York: Ballantine, 1975), p. 139.

Book with CORPORATE AUTHOR

[6]United Nations, *Statistical Yearbook, 1978* (New York: United Nations, 1979), p. 91.

Book with NO KNOWN AUTHOR

[7]*Literary Market Place: The Directory of American Book Publishing.* 1976-77 ed. (New York: Bowker, 1976), p. 129.

Book translated from a FOREIGN LANGUAGE

[8]Aleksandr I. Solzhenitsyn, *The First Circle,* trans. Thomas P. Whitney (New York: Harper & Row, 1968), pp. 214-216.

ONE VOLUME of a work in SEVERAL VOLUMES

[9]Mark Sullivan, *Over HEre (1914-1918),* Vol. V of *Our Times* (New York: Scribner, 1972), pp. 457-492.

Work in a COLLECTION by DIFFERENT AUTHORS

[10]Peter Lisca, "The Grapes of Wrath," in *Steinbeck: A Collection of Critical Essays,* ed. Robert Murray Davis (Englewood Cliffs, N.J.: Prentice-Hall, 1972), pp. 76-76.

Work in a COLLECTION by the SAME AUTHOR

[11]Tennessee Williams, "Summer and Smoke," in *Four Plays* (New York: New American Library, 1976), p. 27.

GOVERNMENT PUBLICATION

[12]U.S. Dept. of Agriculture, *Yearbook of Agriculture, 1974: Shopper's Guide,* 93rd Cong., 2nd sess., H. Doc. 93-279 (Washington, D.C.: GPO, 1975), pp. 142-145.

PAMPHLET

[13]Chronicle Guidance Publications, Inc., *Cartoonists: Occupational Brief,* 4th ed. D.O.T. 141 (Moravia, N.Y.: CGP, 1978).

Article in an ENCYCLOPEDIA — UNSIGNED

[15]"Wankel Engine," *Encyclopedia International,* 1979 ed., p. 196.

Article in a PERIODICAL — WEEKLY

[16]"Fanatical Abortion Fight," *Time,* 9 July 1979, pp. 26-27.

Article in a PERIODICAL — MONTHLY

[17]Issac Asimov, "Asimov on Space Colonization," *Science Digest,* Oct., 1978, p. 18.

Article in a WEEKLY PERIODICAL with volume and number given

[18]"AFL-CIO Looks at Economy," *Facts on File*, 40, No. 1051, 29 Feb. 1980, p. 146.

Article in a NEWSPAPER

[19]Jane E. Brody, *"Nutritional Standards for the 80's," New York Times*, City Ed., 19 March 1980, Sec. C, p. 1, cols. 5-6.

> If article is unsigned, start citation with title, "Nutritional Standards . . . "

LETTER TO THE EDITOR

[20]Warren B. Crummett, Letter, *Science*, 107 (1980), 148.

REVIEW

[21]Philip T. Hartung, "The Screen," rev. of *2001: A Space Odyssey*, by Stanley Kubrick, *Commonweal*, 3 May 1968, pp. 207-208.

> If the review is unsigned, begin the citation with the title of the review or, if untitled, simply with "Rev. of . . ." which stands for review of.

Telephone INTERVIEW

[22]Telephone interview with Tatyana Yankelevich, daughter of Andrei Sakharov, 20 Feb. 1980.

personal INTERVIEW

[23]Personal interview with Jane Jones, Art Curator of Museum of Modern Art, 21 Jan. 1980.

sound FILMSTRIP with an AUTHOR

[24]Marion McDaniel and Michael McDaniel, *Redesigning Man: Science and Human Values* (Filmstrip) New York: Harper & Row Media Program, 1974) with cassettes.

sound FILMSTRIP with NO AUTHOR

[25]"Robert Frost" (Filmstrip), in *The American Experience in Literature: Poets of the 20th Century* (Chicago: Encyclopedia Britannica Educ. Corp., 1976) with cassette.

ART PRINT

[26]Claude Monet, *Boats at Argenteuil* (Print) (U.S.A.: Shorewood Press, Inc., n.d.).

SLIDE

[27]*Surrealism* (Slide) (Stamford, Ct.: Educational Dimensions, 1974).

MICROFORM

[28]"Watch Out for Foot Poisoning" (Microfilm) *Changing Times, Aug. 1975, pp. 36-38.*

MOTION PICTURE

[29]*The Food Revolution* (Motion Picture) (New York: McGraw-Hill, 1968).

sound RECORDING or CASSETTE

[30]Walt Whitman, *Leaves of Grass* (Sound Recording), Ed Begley, reader. (Caedmon n.d. disc TC 1037).

VIDEO TAPE RECORDING (Unpublished) or VIDEOCASSETTE

[31]Pamela Wolfe, "Pam Wolfe Bakes Bread" (Videorecording), presented at Greenwich High School, 1977, cassette.

SAMPLE FOOTNOTE PAGE

[1]Donald Barlow Stauffer, *A Short History of American Poetry* (New York: E.P. Dutton, 1974), p. 173.

[2]Arthur S. Link and William B. Catton, *American Epoch: A History of the United States Since 1890* (New York: Knopf, 1963), p. 502.

[3]United Nations, *Statistical Yearbook, 1978* (New York: United Nations, 1979), p. 91.

[4]Aleksandr Solzhenitsyn, *Warning to the West* (New York: Farrar, Straus & Giroux, 1976), p. 27.

[5]Mark Sullivan, *Over Here (1914-1918), Vol. V of Our Times* (New York: Scribner, 1972), pp. 457-475.

[6]Sullivan, P. 483.

Use this form when citing different pages in the same book by an author.

[7]*Aleksandr I. Solzhenitsyn, The First Circle,* trans. Thomas P. Whitney (New York: Harper & Row, 1968), pp. 214-216.

[8]Ellsworth Raymond, "Energy," *Encyclopedia Americana,* 1979 ed., pp. 341-345.

[9]Solzhenitsyn, *Warning,* p. 40.

When using more than one book by the same author, use the shortened form of the titles for subsequent notes. This example shows a second note for the Solzhenitsyn book, *Warning to the West,* already cited in full.

CHAPTER

11

PREPARING YOUR FINAL DRAFT

After all these weeks of researching, writing (and worrying), the moment of truth is at hand. You are ready to complete your final draft and submit your term paper to your teacher.

Hopefully, you are not reading this (or writing your paper) at three o'clock of the morning your paper is due.

You will need a clear head to successfully negotiate this final step of the term paper process.

If you followed our "kitchen sink" formula, your first draft was excessively long and you had the luxury to delete some of your weaker material. That tightened editing, together with your sense of the strength and flow of the paper, should have produced the basis for a "no nonsense" final draft.

Although the old saying, "too many cooks can spoil the broth," is essentially true, if you have a trusted friend with the time and desire to help you succeed, his or her input (if it is given without bias) could be helpful, as well.

This is your last chance to pay attention to all of the "small" details which can make the difference between an ordinary grade and an extraordinary one.

These details include making sure that the length of the paper meets the teacher's instructions, that the title is as strong and straightforward as it can be, and that you haven't inserted too many footnotes or too many quotations or too many "five dollar" words in an attempt to make the paper feel "more scholarly."

Some students occasionally confuse knowledge and information with pretension. Experienced teachers typically do not appreciate such posture, and have been known to inflict significant penalities on such papers (mainly to forcefully remind the student that they should not employ that transparent approach in the future).

Finally, there comes a moment when you simply have to STOP and make the transition from student to secretary. You've done all you can as the writer of the term paper, and now you're the typist who is simply transcribing the assignment into its final form.

Another reason we hope that you're not reading this (or typing your final draft) at three o'clock of the morning the paper is due is because your final draft has to be a neat, clean copy, free of typographical errors.

Neatness may not count on some sweepstakes entries, but it certainly matters on term papers.

Your paper's appearance has to be as crisp and clear as its contents.

A Final Draft Checklist

If you are writing your paper by hand, many of the details of this section will not pertain to you.

In the event that you are writing by hand, make certain to use only black or blue-black ink, and to write legibly on ruled theme paper.

Most papers, however, are machine-produced and this checklist is directed to the majority of students who do not write their term papers by hand.

(1) You can use a computer printer or a word processor as well as a typewriter. However, if you use a printer or processor, it is best to use one with letter-quality printing.

(2) Use a fresh black ribbon for clear impressions.

(3) Use a 20-pound bond white paper with some rag content. If your printer cannot accommodate such a sheet, then use the best quality paper available for that machine.

(4) If your teacher has indicated that you must follow a proscribed format, then make certain that you are following it. If you have not been given specific instructions, then those included on this checklist should be helpful.

(5) Your title page should include the title of the paper, your name, the name of the course, and the date.

(6) The title page is not numbered. The first page of the paper (which will center the title in capital letters at the top of the page) is numbered at the bottom, and all other pages are numbered on top. Bottom numbers are usually centered; top numbers can be centered or

placed in the upper right-hand corner.

(7) Your top, bottom and right-hand margins should be one-inch (1″) from the edge of the paper; your left-hand margin should be one-and-a-half inches (1½″).

(8) Your paper should be double-spaced throughout except that the footnotes, the bibliography and any long blocks of quotations should be single-spaced.

(9) For the final step of your final draft, make certain that you have the time to carefully proofread the entire paper. This will be your last chance to affect your paper; as we've already observed, neatness *does* count.

CHAPTER 12
THE SECRET OF HANDING IN A WINNING TERM PAPER

If this were a two-way interactive video instead of a one-way book, we would flash a PAUSE up on the screen, suggesting that we hold off on this chapter until you get your term paper back.

Chances are that you'll feel so good that you'll offer to write this chapter in our place.

At the very least, we hope that you feel that we kept our promise: that the process of producing a term paper can be virtually painless and occasionally even pleasureable.

The "secret" turns out to be TLC, that well-known acronym for "tender loving care."

TLC, in its original definition, would probably hold up as well as our modified definition for term papers:

T — Time. You must put in the requisite hours.

L — Labor. You can't take shortcuts and expect success.

C — Commitment. If you become committed and passionate about your paper, that energy will kindle equivalent reciprocity on the part of your teacher.

One final (cheerful) thought: It will be easier next time!

DIRECTORY

BASIC REFERENCE SOURCES

This concise list of basic reference sources is designed to provide you with some of the materials which might prove helpful as you begin working on your term paper assignment.

This list, which is brief and selective, will help you in two ways: (1) As a source of general information, such as that provided by encyclopedias and yearbooks. (2) As a source of more specific information in some of the areas which are common term paper subjects.

It has simply been designed to serve as a catalyst for your own further in-depth research, and is not a bibliography of term paper references or intended to serve as a substitute for the independent research which every successful term paper requires.

Art

American Art Dictionary. New York: R. R. Bowker.

Art Through The Ages. Helen Gardner. New York: Harcourt, Brace.

How To Find Out About The Arts: A Guide To Sources Of Information. Neville Carrick. New York: Pergamon Press.

Guide to Art Reference Books. Mary W. Chamberlin. Chicago: American Library Association.

Encyclopedia of World Art. New York: McGraw-Hill.

The Oxford Companion to Art. Harold Osborne. London: Oxford University Press.

Who's Who in American Art. New York: R. R. Bowker.

Atlases

Encyclopaedia Britannica World Atlas. Chicago: Encyclopaedia Britannica.

Hammond's Contemporary World Atlas. New York: Doubleday.

National Geographic Atlas of the World. Washington, D.C.: National Geographic Society.

The International Atlas. Chicago: Rand, McNally & Co.

Bibliographies

The Bibliographic Index: A Cumulative Bibliography of Bibliographies. New York: H. W. Wilson.

Guide to Reference Books. Constance M. Winchell. Chicago: American Library Association.

Guide to Reference Materials. A. J. Walford. London: Library Association.

A World Bibliography of Bibliographies. Theodore Besterman. Lausanne: Societas Bibliographica.

Biographies

Chamber's Biographical Dictionary. New York: St. Martin's Press.

Current Biography. New York: H. W. Wilson.

Encyclopedia of American Biography. New York: Harper & Row.

The New York Times Obituary Index. New York: New York Times.
Who's Who Series. Chicago: Marquis.

Biology

The Dictionary of the Biological Sciences. New York: Reinhold.
Encyclopedia of the Biological Sciences. New York: Van Nostrand-Reinhold.

Chemistry

Chemical Publications: Their Nature and Use. Melvin G. Mellon. New York: McGraw-Hill.
Encyclopedia of Chemistry. New York: Van Nostrand-Reinhold.

Dictionaries

American Heritage Dictionary of the English Language. Boston: Houghton Mifflin.
Oxford English Dictionary. Oxford: Clarendon Press.
Random House Dictionary of the English Language. New York: Random House.
Webster's Third New International Dictionary of the English Language. Springfield, Mass.: G.&C. Merriam.

Economics

McGraw-Hill Dictionary of Modern Economics. New York: McGraw-Hill.
Economics: An Introductory Analysis. Paul Anthony Samuelson. New York: McGraw-Hill.
World Economic Survey. New York: United Nations.

Encyclopedias

Chamber's Encyclopedia. London: International Learning Systems Corp.
Collier's Encyclopedia. New York: Crowell-Collier Educational Corp.

The New Columbia Encyclopedia. New York: Columbia University Press.
Encyclopedia Americana. New York: Americana Corp.
Encyclopaedia Britannica. Chicago: Encyclopaedia Britannica, Inc.

History

Cambridge Ancient History. New York: Macmillan.
Cambridge Medieval History. New York: Macmillan.
Cambridge Modern History. New York: Macmillan.
Encyclopedia of American History. New York: Harper & Row.
Guide to Historical Literature. American Historical Association. New York: Macmillan.
The Oxford Companion to American History. Thomas H. Johnson. New York: Oxford University Press.
Western Europe: A Handbook. New York: Praeger.

Literature

American Authors: 1600-1900. Stanley J. Kunitz and Howard Haycraft. New York: H. W. Wilson.
Cassell's Encyclopedia of World Literature. New York: Morrow.
The Oxford Companion to American Literature. James D. Hart. New York: Oxford University Press.
The Oxford Companion to Classical Literature. Sir Paul Harvey. New York: Clarendon Press.
The Oxford Companion to English Literature. Sir Paul Harvey. Oxford: Clarendon Press.
The Oxford Companion to French Literature. Sir Paul Harvey & Janet E. Heseltine. Oxford: Clarendon Press.
Twentieth Century Authors: A Biographical Dictionary of Modern Literature. Stanley J. Kunitz. New York: H. W. Wilson.

Philosophy

Encyclopedia of Philosophy. Paul Edwards. New York: Macmillan.
A History of Philosophy. Wilhelm Windelband. New York: Harper Torch Books.

A History of Western Philosophy. Bertrand Russell. New York: Simon & Schuster.
The Philosopher's Index: An International Index to Philosophical Periodicals. Bowling Green, Ohio: Bowling Green University.

Political Science

Dictionary of American Politics. Edward C. Smith and Arnold J. Zurcher. New York: Barnes & Noble.
Guide to the Study of International Relations. Janusz Zawodny. San Francisco: Chandler.
The Literature of Political Science: A Guide for Students, Librarians & Teachers. Clifton Brock. New York: R. R. Bowker.
The Major Political Systems of Europe. New York: Random House.

Psychology

A Dictionary of Psychology. Baltimore: Penguin Books.
Contributions to Modern Psychology: Selected Readings in General Psychology. New York: Oxford University Press.
The Harvard List of Books in Psychology. Cambridge, Mass.: Harvard University Press.
Introduction to Psychology. Clifford T. Morgan. New York: McGraw-Hill.

Religion

Cambridge History of the Bible. Cambridge: Cambridge University Press.
Encyclopaedia Judaica. New York: Macmillan.
Encyclopedia of Religion & Ethics. New York: Scribner.
The New Catholic Encyclopedia. Catholic University of America. New York: McGraw-Hill.
A Reader's Guide to the Great Religions. Charles J. Adams. New York: Free Press.

Science and Technology

Applied Science and Technology Index. New York: H. W. Wilson.

Science and Technology: An Introduction to the Literature. Denis J. Grogan. Hamden, Conn.: Archon Books.
Van Nostrand's Scientific Encyclopedia. Princeton, N.J.: Van Nostrand.

Sociology

Dictionary of Modern Sociology. Thomas F. Hoult. Totowa, N.J.: Littlefield, Adams and Company.
International Bibliography of Sociology. Chicago: Aldine.
Sociology Today: Problems and Prospects. Robert K. Merton. New York: Basic Books.

Social Sciences

Dictionary of the Social Sciences. New York: Crowell-Collier.
International Encyclopedia of the Social Sciences. New York: Macmillan.
Social Sciences and Humanities Index. New York: H. W. Wilson.

Yearbooks

Americana Annual. New York: Americana Corp.
The Annual Register of World Events. London: Longmans.
Britannica Book of the Year. Chicago: Encyclopaedia Britannica.
Information Please Almanac. New York: Information Please Almanac.
World Almanac & Book of Facts. New York: Newspaper Enterprise Association.

GLOSSARY OF ABBREVIATIONS

As you become more involved in the research process, you will come across abbreviations which may be unfamiliar to you.

This selected glossary has been prepared with a view towards providing you with comprehensive definitions of some of the more commonly used abbreviations.

anon. — anonymous
app. — appendix
assn. — association
art. — article
b. — born
bibliog. — bibliography
bk. — book
b&w — black and white
ca. — about
City Ed. — City Edition (of a newspaper)

col.	—	column
comp.	—	compiled by
d.	—	died
ed.	—	edited, editor
e.g.	—	for example
encyc.	—	encyclopedia
ERIC	—	Educational Resources Information Center
esp.	—	especially
et al.	—	and others
fac.	—	facsimile
fig.	—	figure
fn.	—	footnote
GPO	—	Government Printing Office, Washington, D.C.
H. Doc.	—	House Document
H.R.	—	House of Representatives
ibid.	—	ibidem ("in the same place"), meaning the title cited in the note directly before.
i.e.	—	that is
illus.	—	illustrated, illustration
in.	—	inches
lang.	—	language
loc. cit.	—	in the place cited
min.	—	minutes
mm	—	millimeter (8, 16 or 35) of film
n.b.	—	note well
n.d.	—	no date
n.n.	—	no name
n.p.	—	no place of publication, or publisher
no.	—	number

op. cit.	—	opere citato ("in the work cited"), meaning a title referred to again after other notes have intervened.
p.	—	page
pp.	—	pages
par.	—	paragraph
pseud.	—	pseudonym
pub.	—	published, publication
q.v.	—	which see
rev. of	—	review of
rev.	—	revised
rpm	—	revolutions per minute
S.	—	Senate
S. Doc.	—	Senate Document
sec.	—	section
sd.	—	sound
ser.	—	series
sess.	—	session
sig.	—	signature
sp.	—	space
trans.	—	translator, translated
univ.	—	university
verso.	—	back of the title page
vol.	—	volume
vols.	—	volumes

DIRECTORY

50 REGIONAL DEPOSITORY LIBRARIES FOR U.S. GOVERNMENT PUBLICATIONS

The most prolific publisher in the United States is . . . the United States! In fact, the Federal Government publishes thousands of books, pamphlets and reports each year. Many of them can prove useful to a student in search of current, authoritative information.

Virtually every public and school library in the country contains some U.S. Government publications.

Fifty libraries, designated as Regional Depository Libraries for U.S. Government publications, contain virtually everything which the Government publishes. If you live near one, or can visit it without any great effort or expense, the Regional Directory Library closest to you may prove to be a valuable source of information.

ALABAMA	Auburn University Library Montgomery (205) 271-9621
	University of Alabama Library Birmingham (205) 934-8221
ARIZONA	Department of Library State Capitol Phoenix (602) 255-4121
	University of Arizona Library Tucson (602) 621-3237
ARKANSAS	Arkansas State Library Little Rock (501) 371-1524
CALIFORNIA	California State Library Sacramento (916) 322-4570
COLORADO	University of Colorado Library Boulder (303) 492-1224
	Denver Public Library Denver (303) 571-2000

CONNECTICUT	Connecticut State Library Hartford (203) 566-4777
FLORIDA	University of Florida Library Gainesville (904) 392-1365
GEORGIA	University of Georgia Library Athens (404) 542-2112
HAWAII	University of Hawaii Library Honolulu (808) 948-8975
IDAHO	University of Idaho Library Moscow (208) 885-6326
ILLINOIS	Illinois State Library Springfield (217) 782-2994
INDIANA	Indiana State Library Indianapolis (317) 232-3675
IOWA	University of Iowa Library Iowa City (319) 335-3847

KANSAS	University of Kansas Library Lawrence (913) 864-3911
KENTUCKY	University of Kentucky Library Lexington (606) 257-7148
LOUISIANA	Louisiana State University Library Baton Rouge (504) 388-1231
	Louisiana Tech University Library Ruston (318) 257-3036
MAINE	University of Maine Library Orono (207) 581-1561
MARYLAND	University of Maryland Library College Park (301) 454-5550
MASSACHUSETTS	Boston Public Library Boston (617) 536-5400

MICHIGAN	Detroit Public Library Detroit (313) 833-1000
	Michigan State University Library East Lansing (517) 355-8332
MINNESOTA	University of Minnesota Library Duluth (218) 726-7171
MISSISSIPPI	University of Mississippi Library University (601) 232-7226
MONTANA	University of Montana Library Missoula (406) 243-6266
NEBRASKA	Nebraska Library Commission Lincoln (402) 471-2045
NEVADA	University of Nevada Library Reno (702) 784-6865
NEW JERSEY	Newark Public Library Newark (201) 733-7800

NEW MEXICO	University of New Mexico Library Albuquerque (505) 277-7575
	New Mexico State Library Santa Fe (505) 827-3800
NEW YORK	New York State Library Albany (518) 474-7646
NORTH CAROLINA	University of North Carolina Library Chapel Hill (919) 966-3621
NORTH DAKOTA	University of North Dakota Library Grand Forks (701) 777-3821
OHIO	State Library of Ohio Columbus (614) 644-7061

OKLAHOMA	Oklahoma Department of Libraries Oklahoma City (405) 521-2502
	Oklahoma State University Library Stillwater (405) 624-6857
OREGON	Portland State University Library Portland (503) 464-3511
PENNSYLVANIA	State Library of Pennsylvania Harrisburg (717) 787-4440
TEXAS	Texas State Library Austin (512) 463-5455
	Texas Tech University Library Lubbock (806) 742-3661
UTAH	Utah State University Library Logan (801) 750-1124
VIRGINIA	University of Virginia Library Charlottesville (804) 924-7751

WASHINGTON	Washington State Library Olympia (206) 753-5590
WEST VIRGINIA	West Virginia University Library Morgantown (304) 293-2124
WISCONSIN	Milwaukee Public Library Milwaukee (414) 278-3000
	State Historical Library of Wisconsin Madison (608) 262-9590
WYOMING	Wyoming State Library Cheyenne (307) 777-7281

ABOUT THE AUTHOR

Steve Kahn is an attorney and publishing entrepreneur. He is the creator and author of the *No Nonsense Success Guides* and, now, the *No Nonsense Study Guides.* He holds a B.S. degree from New York University and a J.D. degree from New York Law School. He was assisted in the development of the *No Nonsense Study Guides* by his wife, who holds a B.A. degree from Barnard College and an M.F.A. degree from Columbia University, and by his son, who is currently attending a prominent college in quest of his B.A. degree in Political Science.

ABOUT THE NO NONSENSE STUDY SERIES

The *No Nonsense Study Guides* have been created in response to a growing need for basic and useful information for students and their families. The successful *No Nonsense* "system" is uniquely positioned to deliver such information in an efficient, educational and entertaining format. Look for this related *No Nonsense Study Guide:* **The Parent-Student Guide To Selecting Colleges & Universities.**